THE HUMAN BODY

THE BRAIN

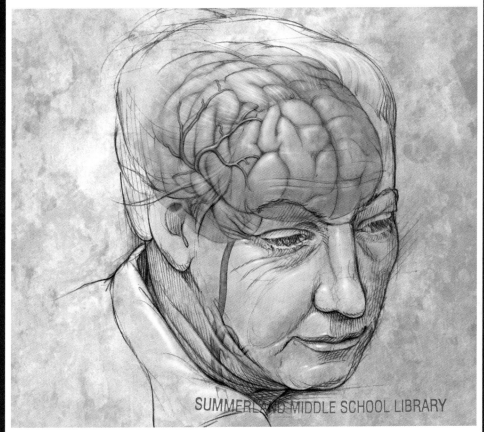

By Susan H. Gray

THE CHILD'S WORLD®
CHANHASSEN, MINNESOTA

The Child's World

Published in the United States of America by The Child's World
PO Box 326, Chanhassen, MN 55317-0326
800-599-READ
www.childsworld.com

Content Adviser:
R. John Solaro,
PhD, Distinguished
University Professor
Head, Department
of Physiology and
Biophysics, University
of Illinois at Chicago

Photo Credits: Cover/frontispiece: Photodisc. Interior: Corbis: 5 (Richard T. Nowitz), 16 (Lester V. Bergman); Custom Medical Stock Photo: 8, 13 (B. Cox); Getty Images: 11 (Photodisc/Michael Matisse), 19 (Taxi/Jim Cummins); Getty Images/The Image Bank: 10 (Joseph Devenney), 23 (Gary S. and Vivian Chapman); Getty Images/Stone: 7 (Chris Everard), 15 (Ron Boardman); PhotoEdit: 24 (Jeff Greenburg), 25 (Jonathan Nourok); David Young-Wolff/PhotoEdit: 17, 27.

The Child's World: Mary Berendes, Publishing Director

Editorial Directions, Inc.: E. Russell Primm, Editorial Director; Pam Rosenberg, Editor; Katie Marsico, Associate Editor; Judith Shiffer, Assistant Editor; Matt Messbarger, Editorial Assistant; Susan Hindman, Copy Editor; Sarah E. De Capua, Proofreader; Judith Frisbie, Peter Garnham, Olivia Nellums, Chris Simms, Fact Checkers; Tim Griffin/IndexServ, Indexer; Cian Loughlin O'Day, Photo Researcher; Linda S. Koutris, Photo Editor

The Design Lab: Kathleen Petelinsek, Design; Kari Thornborough, Production Design

Library of Congress Cataloging-in-Publication Data
Gray, Susan Heinrichs.
  The brain / by Susan H. Gray.
      p. cm. — (The human body)
  Includes index.
  ISBN 1-59296-424-9 (library bound : alk. paper) 1. Brain—Juvenile literature. I. Title.
  QP361.5.G69 2005
  612.8'2—dc22   2005000569

TABLE OF CONTENTS

CHAPTER ONE

GIVE IT A REST!

Matthew fell asleep as soon as his head hit the pillow. He had stayed up late the night before, and then he'd gotten up early for his soccer game. After soccer, he mowed the lawn, helped his dad with some chores, and ate supper. He could barely keep his eyes open while he ate. After supper, he took a quick shower and tumbled into bed.

All day long, Matt's brain had been in high gear. It allowed Matt to kick the soccer ball and run without losing his balance. It guided his movements as he mowed the grass. At supper, it told him when he was full. At the end of this long day, his brain needed a rest.

Your brain doesn't stop working when you sleep. It is still coordinating breathing and other activities that happen all the time, even when you aren't thinking about them.

CHAPTER TWO

WHAT IS THE BRAIN?

The brain is the control center of the body and the main **organ** of the nervous system. It works with the spinal cord and the nerves to pick up information from the **environment** and to make the body respond.

The brain is a soft organ in the skull. The spinal cord is a thick bundle of nerves that starts at the base of the brain and runs down the back. It is protected by the backbone. The nerve cells, or neurons (NOOR-onz), are the body's "wiring." They make up the **tissues** of the brain and spinal cord, and they also extend into almost every other body tissue.

At their endings, the nerves pick up messages from the environment, both outside and inside the body. For example, nerve endings in

Have you ever eaten a hamburger that was this big? Were you able to eat the whole thing before your stomach's nerve endings sent signals to your brain telling it that your stomach was full?

the skin sense heat, cold, touch, pressure, and pain. Nerves in the

stomach sense when that organ has **expanded** too much. These

signals then travel along the nerves to the spinal cord or brain. There,

the messages jump to other nerves.

Neurons in the brain **interpret** the messages and decide how the body should respond. That signal runs from the brain, back down the spinal cord, along the nerves, and out to the body.

Your spinal cord runs down the middle of your back. It is the pathway that connects your brain to every nerve cell in your body.

For example, nerve endings in your foot might pick up the signal that you've stepped on something and can't pull away. Neurons carry that signal up your leg, then up your spinal cord, and to your brain. Neurons in your brain interpret the signal. They figure out that you've stepped on something sticky. Your brain decides that you need to lift up your foot higher. That message runs from your brain, down your spinal cord, and to your leg. Leg muscles react, causing your foot to raise before you can think of doing this.

At the same time, other neurons in your brain decide that you need to bend your head down so you can look at your foot. That message shoots out of your brain to your neck muscles, and you bend your head. You use your eyes to look at the bottom of your foot. You see a pink, gooey mess. Nerves from your eyes send that signal to your brain. The brain interprets the mess as gum. Your

Picking up your foot to see what you've stepped in seems simple, but it requires your brain to coordinate the activity of a lot of different muscles and nerves.

brain then sends a nerve message to your lips and vocal cords, and

you use your mouth to say, "Yuck!"

This scene shows how nerves all over the body send messages

to the brain. Neurons in the brain figure out the meaning of the

messages. They also decide what the body should do next. Finally,

they send commands out to the different body parts, telling them

how to respond.

CHAPTER THREE

WHAT PARTS MAKE
UP THE BRAIN?

Four main parts make up the brain. These are the cerebrum (suh-REE-brum), the cerebellum (SEHR-uh-BELL-um), the brain stem, and the diencephalon (die-en-SEFF-uh-lon). The cerebrum is the largest part of the brain. It is divided into right and

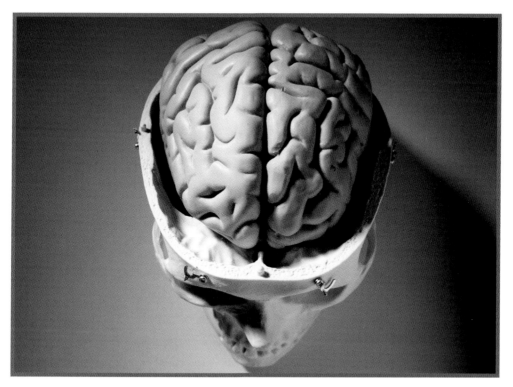

The cerebrum is the largest part of the human brain, making up about two-thirds of its weight. If you could lift off the top of your skull and look at your cerebrum, it would look a lot like this.

left halves by a deep **groove.** The cerebrum is gray and has many folds and **creases.**

The cerebellum is about the size of your fist and lies under the back part of the cerebrum. It is also gray, divided into two sides, and covered with folds and creases. The brain stem is directly in front of the cerebellum. It is white and smooth and connects to the spinal cord.

The fourth part of the brain, the diencephalon, is buried deep within the tissues of the cerebrum. It includes some small—but very important—parts of the brain.

The entire brain is surrounded by the bones of the skull. Just inside the skull, there is a layer of fat and three tissue layers with fluid-filled spaces between them. The skull bones, tissues, fat, and fluid protect and cushion the brain.

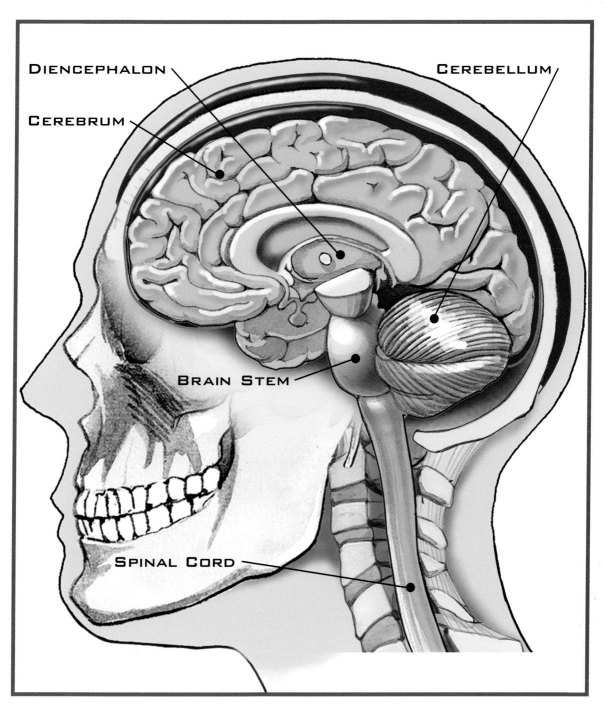

DIENCEPHALON

CEREBELLUM

CEREBRUM

BRAIN STEM

SPINAL CORD

Your brain is made up of four main parts, pictured above.
Your spinal cord connects your brain to the rest of your body.

CHAPTER FOUR

WHAT KINDS OF CELLS ARE IN THE BRAIN?

There are two main types of cells in the brain—neurons and glial (GLEE-uhl) cells, which are often simply called glia (GLEE-uh). The human brain contains about 100 billion neurons and at least twice as many glia. These two cell types have very different jobs.

Neurons in the brain are much like neurons everywhere else in the nervous system. They have three main parts—the dendrites (DEN-drites), the cell body, and the axon (AX-on). Dendrites are short, hairlike branches at the end of a nerve. They pick up signals from the environment and send them electrically to the cell body. The cell body is an enlarged part of the nerve cell and is sometimes shaped like a star. It keeps the cell alive by processing oxygen and **nutrients.**

Magnified many times through a microscope, axons from a human spinal cord look like this.

Electrical signals move from the cell body down the length of the

axon. At the end of the axon, the signal jumps to the dendrites of the

next nerve. In this way, signals travel from neuron to neuron. The

signals reach the brain and spread to other neurons, which then

interpret their meaning.

Neurons are important, but they couldn't begin to do their work

without glia. Scientists used to think that glia were nothing more than

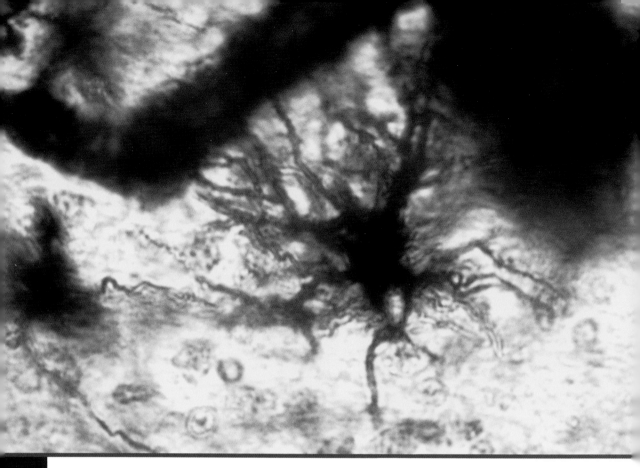

These glial cells are wrapped around capillaries, the tiny blood vessels that carry oxygen and nutrients to every cell in your body.

the packing material surrounding neurons. In recent years, however, they have found that glia have very important jobs.

Some glia feed neurons. They pick up nutrients from the blood and pass them to nearby neurons. Other glia destroy germs that attack neurons. Still other glia form a fatty coating around nerve cells. This coating helps neurons to conduct their signals properly.

CHAPTER FIVE

WHAT DO THE CEREBRUM AND CEREBELLUM DO?

Every part of the brain has its own job to do. The cerebrum receives signals related to heat, cold, and touch.

It interprets those signals and then tells the body how to move in

The nerve endings in this person's hand are sending signals to the cerebrum that let it know that the ice cubes are cold. When the person's hand becomes too cold, his brain will send signals back to the muscles in the hand with a message—Let go!

response to them. The cerebrum also picks up messages from the ears, eyes, nose, and mouth. It then interprets those sounds, sights, smells, and tastes. In addition, it controls the movements of the eyes, face, and tongue.

Nerves in the cerebrum control our ability to speak and understand language. They are responsible for our emotions, and they help us memorize and remember things. They also help us solve problems and make decisions. These nerve activities are not well understood, but we certainly could not live without them.

The cerebellum, or "little brain," works closely with the cerebrum. When nerves from the cerebrum tell muscles in the body to move, nerves from the cerebellum add their input. Thanks to this input, the body's movements are smooth and coordinated. The cerebellum also helps us control our posture and balance.

*The cerebellum works with the cerebrum to help this quarterback
keep his balance and throw the ball accurately.*

During the 1860s, America was involved in a bloody civil war. Silas Weir Mitchell (far right) was a surgeon and treated soldiers with horrible injuries. He often had to remove soldiers' limbs and then help them to get better.

As the soldiers began to heal, they told Dr. Mitchell some strange stories. They said they still had feelings in their arms and legs, even though these limbs were gone. They said their legs itched, their hands were cold, or their boots were too tight. Dr. Mitchell puzzled over these stories, but he could not explain them. He did, however, give the problem a name. He said the soldiers had feelings in their "phantom limbs."

Since that time, doctors have heard phantom limb stories quite often. Most people who have some part of their body removed during surgery—even if it's as small as a little finger—will say they still have feelings in that part. Some report painful feelings such as pinpricks, while others say they have very pleasant feelings. But how is that possible?

Some doctors believe that the brain is partly responsible for the phantom feelings. For example, they say that a certain brain area is used to receiving signals from the left hand. When the left hand is no longer there, that brain area misses the signals. It takes a while, but the brain reorganizes itself to make up for the missing signals. After it reorganizes, it receives signals from another area nearby. But the brain often interprets these signals incorrectly and thinks they still come from the hand.

The brain area that receives signals from the hand is near the area that receives signals from the face. When a doctor touches the face of a patient who has lost a hand, that patient may say he

feels something touching his hand. It seems that the brain is picking up signals from the face and running them through the area that used to get signals from the hand. Therefore, the brain thinks that the hand is being touched, even though it is no longer there.

Of course, this does not explain everything about phantom limb feelings. But it shows how complex the brain is and how much we still have to learn.

CHAPTER SIX

WHAT ABOUT THE DIENCEPHALON AND BRAIN STEM?

The diencephalon contains nerve tissues that process sights and sounds. It also has neurons that are related to feelings of happiness and sadness. Some areas of the diencephalon tell you when you feel hungry, thirsty, full, sleepy, or alert. Others help to keep your body at the proper temperature.

Of all the work the brain does, some of the most important takes place in the brain stem. The centers that control the heart and lungs are located there. So are the centers that control coughing, sneezing, hiccupping, and swallowing. Neurons in the brain stem automatically send signals to regulate the number of beats our hearts make and the number of breaths our lungs

Feelings of sadness are processed in the diencephalon.

When you run, your heart beats faster and your lungs take in more oxygen. Thanks to your brain stem, this happens even though you aren't thinking about your heart and lungs at all.

make each minute without our having to think about it. Brain

stem activities are extremely important, and injuries to this area

often lead to death.

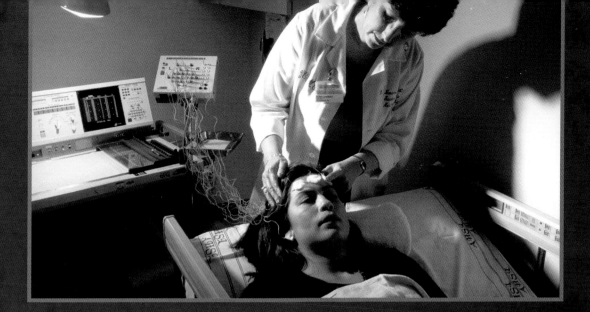

NEVER A DULL MOMENT

Scientists say that we go through five stages as we fall asleep. Stage one is a very light sleep from which we can easily awake. At stages two, three, and four, we sleep more deeply.

At some point in stage four, the brain stem begins to send signals to the diencephalon. The diencephalon sends the signals on to the cerebrum. Then we enter the deepest sleep of all—Rapid Eye Movement (REM) sleep. At this stage, our eyes roll back and forth very quickly, although they are closed. It is during REM sleep that we begin to dream.

Scientists aren't quite sure why people dream. Some believe that the cerebrum uses dreams to make sense of all the signals it has received recently. Additional signals from the brain stem get mixed in, and sometimes the dreams become quite strange.

Even if they can't explain dreams, scientists do know that REM sleep is very important. People who do not get enough often have trouble learning new skills. They also have a hard time remembering new information. Clearly, even when it's resting, the brain is still at work.

CHAPTER SEVEN

WHAT'S NEW WITH THE BRAIN?

Every day, scientists are learning new things about this amazing organ. Studies show that people with healthy glia might not get Alzheimer's (ALTZ-hi-murz) disease. This disease causes people to lose their memory.

Some scientists are trying to find out what happens in the brain that makes people sleepwalk. Others are exploring ways to help people get over their phantom limb pain.

Some doctors are studying people with brain injuries. They have learned that healthy parts of the brain will sometimes take on the jobs of the damaged parts. With this knowledge, doctors can often help their patients recover. The brain is the most complex of all organs. We might not ever discover all of its secrets.

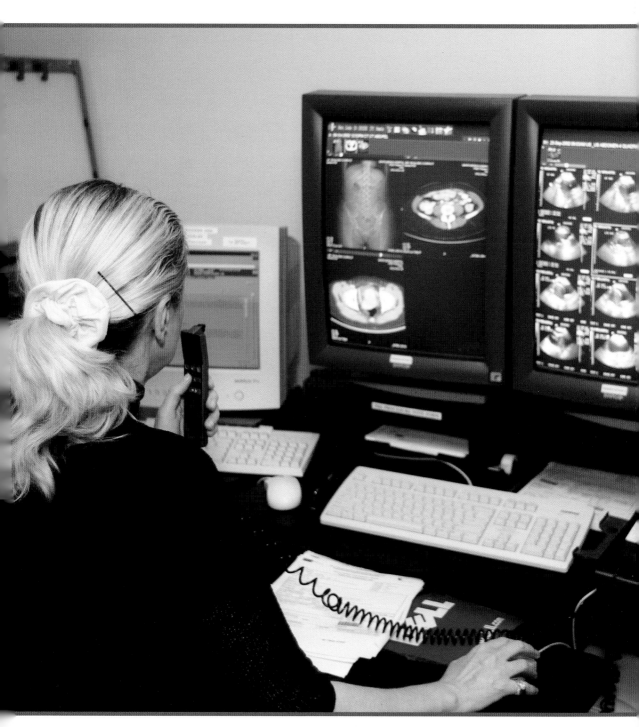

A doctor studies images of a brain as she attempts to learn more about this amazing organ.

Glossary

complex (kom-PLEKS) Something that is complex is complicated. The brain is the most complex of all the organs.

creases (KREESS-ez) Creases are lines or folds. The cerebrum has many creases.

environment (en-VYE-ruhn-muhnt) An environment is made up of the things that surround a person, such as the air, soil, and water. The brain works with the spinal cord and nerves to pick up information from the environment.

expanded (ek-SPAND-ed) Something that has expanded has increased in size. Nerves in the stomach tell us when that organ has expanded too much.

groove (GROOV) A groove is a cut in an object's surface. The cerebrum is divided into two halves by a deep groove.

interpret (in-TUR-prit) To interpret something means to figure out its meaning. Nerves in the brain interpret messages and tell the body how to respond.

nutrients (NOO-tree-uhntz) Nutrients are found in food and are necessary for life and growth. The cell body processes oxygen and nutrients.

organ (OR-guhn) An organ is a body part that performs a certain job. The brain is a soft organ and is located in the skull.

phantom (FAN-tuhm) A phantom is a ghost. During the Civil War, soldiers who lost their arms or legs often experienced feelings in their phantom limbs.

surgeon (SUR-juhn) A surgeon is a doctor who performs operations. Silas Weir Mitchell was a surgeon during the Civil War.

tissues (TISH-ooz) Tissues are groups of similar cells that make up an organ or body part. Nerve cells make up the tissues of the brain and spinal cord.

Questions and Answers about the Brain

My grandmother had a stroke, and now she can't remember certain things. Did something happen to her brain? A stroke occurs when an area of the brain fails to get enough blood and oxygen. If that happens, neurons in that area can no longer function properly and may begin to die. For your grandmother, this probably happened in a memory center of her brain.

Do glial cells exist only in the brain? No, glia exist throughout the entire nervous system. Scientists believe that there are more than 1 trillion of these cells in the body.

I watched my baby brother sleeping, and it seemed like he was making rapid eye movements all the time. Was something wrong with him? No, this was normal for him. When sleeping, infants spend about half their time in REM sleep. As they grow older, they spend less and less time in this stage of deep sleep. Adults usually get less than two hours of REM sleep every night.

Did You Know?

- Together, the brain and spinal cord are often called the Central Nervous System (CNS).

- Sometimes people drink alcohol to help them fall asleep. But alcohol prevents people from reaching the deeper stages of sleep. They do not get the REM sleep they need.

- An adult human brain weighs about 3 pounds (1.3 kilograms).

- The word *diencephalon* means "between brain." It lies between tissues of the cerebrum and the brain stem.

How to Learn More about the Brain

At the Library

Hayhurst, Chris. *The Brain and Spinal Cord: Learning How We Think, Feel, and Move.* New York: Rosen Publishing Group, 2001.

Parker, Steve. *Brain, Nerves, and Senses.* Milwaukee: Gareth Stevens Publishing, 2004.

Walker, Pam, and Elaine Wood. *The Brain and Nervous System.* San Diego: Lucent Books, 2003.

On the Web

Visit our home page for lots of links about the brain:
http://www.childsworld.com/links
Note to Parents, Teachers, and Librarians: We routinely verify our Web links to make sure they're safe, active sites—so encourage your readers to check them out!

Through the Mail or by Phone

AMERICAN ACADEMY FOR CEREBRAL PALSY AND DEVELOPMENTAL MEDICINE
6300 N. River Road, Suite 727
Rosemont, IL 60018-4226
847/698-1635

AMERICAN ACADEMY OF NEUROLOGY
1080 Montreal Avenue
Saint Paul, MN 55116
800/879-1960

MIGRAINE AWARENESS GROUP: A NATIONAL UNDERSTANDING FOR MIGRANEURS
113 S. Saint Asaph Street, Suite 300
Alexandria, VA 22314
703/739-9384

Common Brain Disorders

Cerebral palsy (suh-REE-bruhl PAWL-zee) is caused when a baby's brain does not get enough oxygen at the time of birth. This damages the cerebrum's ability to control muscle movement. A person with cerebral palsy might have some trouble picking up small objects or walking smoothly. Cerebral palsy cannot be cured, but therapy and exercise can help people with this problem.

People who suffer from epilepsy (EP-uh-LEP-see) can blackout or have convulsions, jerky movements of the body's muscles, with little or no warning. These episodes are called seizures. They are caused when the brain's nerve cells don't signal each other properly. Epilepsy can usually be controlled with medicine. In some cases, surgery may help control the seizures.

Migraines (MY-graynz) are severe headaches that usually occur on just one side of the head. Doctors are not sure what causes them, but they think that stress or certain foods might set them off. People usually treat their migraines with drugs made especially for this kind of headache.

Meningitis (men-in-JY-tiss) is an infection or irritation of the thin layers of tissue that cover the brain and spinal cord. People with meningitis often have fever and headaches. The problem can be mild, but severe cases can sometimes lead to death. There are different types of meningitis, and most types can be treated or even prevented with drugs.

Index

About the Author

Susan H. Gray has a bachelor's and a master's degree in zoology, and has taught college-level anatomy and physiology courses. In her twenty-five years as an author, she has written many medical articles, grant proposals, and children's books. Ms. Gray enjoys gardening, traveling, and playing the piano and organ. She has traveled twice to the Russian Far East to give organ workshops to church musicians. She also works extensively with American and Russian friends to develop medical and social service programs for Vladivostok, Russia. Ms. Gray and her husband, Michael, live in Cabot, Arkansas.